TESSA R

Meausa Dozen

and other poems

THE RAMSAY HEAD PRESS
EDINBURGH

Acknowledgements are due to the editors and publishers
of the following journals and periodicals in which
some of these poems have previously appeared:

*Chapman, Cyphers, The Fiddlehead, Northlight, Northwords,
Poetry Ireland, Poetry Wales, The Scotsman, Spectrum, Z20,*
and the anthologies *Meantime* (Polygon 1991) and
Under Cover (Mainstream 1994).

By the same author:

(as Tessa Stiven)
Poetry of Persons (1976)
While it is Yet Day (1977)

(as Tessa Ransford)
Light of the Mind (1980)
Fools and Angels (1984)
Shadows from the Greater Hill (1987)
A Dancing Innocence (1988)
Seven Valleys (1991)

© Tessa Ransford 1994

ISBN 1 873921 03 9

First published in 1994 by
The Ramsay Head Press
15 Gloucester Place
Edinburgh EH3 6EE

*The publisher acknowledges subsidy from
The Scottish Arts Council towards the
publication of this volume
and the Financial assistance of
The Deric Bolton Poetry Trust.*

Printed in Scotland by W. M. Bett, Tillicoultry

Contents

MEDUSA DOZEN

Medusa Dozen, *thirteen poems* 5

EXCHANGE OF DREAMS

The Willows and the Vines 17
Buddha in Europe 19
Monks in Black and White 21
To My Son Going Abroad 22
Floating People 23
Burden 26
Set Loose 27
Vineyard in Winter 28
Chanticleer 29
Laura 30
Le Carrousel 31
Thunder in Vaucluse 34
Rose Window, Vincennes 36
Exchange of Dreams 37
Golden Images 38

ROUGH BOUNDS

Rough Bounds 39
Viewpoint 40
The Shetland Fiddler 41
The Clarsach 42
Carried Away 43
Travelling on Music 48
To the Swift 49
The Wall and the Tree 51
Parable 53
An Easter 54
Evensong *(May)* 55

Winter Day in the Borders 56
First Thaw 57
Gorse Girl 58
A Scented Garden 59
Working Mind 60

SLOW EMOTION

Poetry Goes Through Walls 61
Carmina Gadelica in Australia 62
Force Fields 63
Navigare Necesse Est 64
Transverberation, *sequence of seven sonnets* 65
Slow Emotion 69
Shiatsu 70
Black Hara 70
Kamakura 71
Sanjusangendo 72
Brave 73
Caprice 74
Not in a Garden 75
What More 77
Regeneration 78
Shrine 79
Driving Through Tweeddale 79

Medusa Dozen

A sequence of thirteen poems invoking Medusa, who was a serpent-goddess, ruler, healer, destroyer, awe-ful and sublime in her extreme holiness. Medusa's head was on Athene's shield. A female face surrounded by serpent hair was an ancient, widely-recognised symbol of sacred wisdom, feminine intelligence. The Greek legend tells that Medusa turned men to stone (petrified them) and that Perseus beheaded her, looking at her image in a mirror shield. (Samson and Delilah could be a transposed version of the story, where the man has as it were stolen the feminine secret strength by never cutting his hair).

The number thirteen (for the thirteen moons) must have been a sacred and lucky one in fertility religions, converted to an unlucky one when these were overthrown, but surviving in the "baker's dozen".

William Blake's maxim informs the whole: "Without contraries is no progression. Attraction and repulsion, reason and energy, love and hate are necessary to human existence".

Medusa One

Delicate as the thread given us for the dark
to slay, not our invisible
circulating holiness
but the monstrous will to power
that blocks our healing flow.

It is the clue by which we feel our way
descend to the unconscious
as the egg to the womb.

Follow this narrow path that mazes
upon itself. Do not break the thread.
Assemble the broken pieces of your dream.

If you could dream of me
I would unfurl
like a flower at speed
and blossom in the rainbow
of contradiction.

If you dreamt of me by day
you would recognise me at night
you would know the light of my countenance.

Medusa Two

I do not see red I see black.
It is his point of view
in heavy black type.

His arguments are clearly presented.
I make no mistake.
I see them black against
a wall of noncommittal.

I know but do not feel
his side of the question.
What I feel is my own
my own point of view
my web of words
my sea-green underworld.

We breathe in a different element
and make each other gasp.

※　　※　　※

I shine like gorse:
each petal an atom of sun
with its own radiation.

I shine like that
brilliant and gilding the hillside.

But my flare is for revenge:
against no person but
against the imposition.

Medusa Three

Not stringency of just laws
but principles of our nature
like "blessed are the meek"
for nourishment of the least
and protection of each strand
in the woven-unwoven cosmos.

Penelope was not patient
but reliable and kept
her world in holiness
her systems renewable.

It is not that we grow weary —
for each effort forwards us
in the sway of its own momentum
to sustain the pattern we make
by slight gestures, in few words,
with the habit of attention
to what we think we feel.

Medusa Four

Is it too late for me to win your love,
the love I thought you wanted me to keep
but that you somehow never gave? I let
myself believe this thing I seemed to hold.
My hands encradled what imagination
first presumed to be your gift of love.

But then their emptiness would make me raise
them to my head, to batter disillusion
with pain into my skull, while looking down
my own gifts poured unwanted from my thighs.

Is it too late for you to once admit
to feelings that enhance you by their strength?
Your dignity in hoarding them is less.
We cannot give what we do not possess,
but in this matter what we have is only
in proportion to the love we give.
Mutual interflowing is the real.
It means a risk of losing everything
for nothing in return, or else for all:
all that is of life its own perfection.

Medusa Five

The man I love has turned to stone.
He may have seen the snakes in my head.
Now he cannot look at me
or touch. He finds my serpents
dangerous, their true imagining.

Blood vessels in my brain have turned
to writhing snakes. Tensed, then dilated,
they throb and twist and stretch and hiss.
They are killed by hammering
with clubs, until I retch and cannot move.

The answer was to cut off
my head from connection to the nerves.
No messages, no sudden strike;
to knock senseless, block signals,
put the lid on iridescent serpents.

The man I love is petrified.
He never looks directly at me now
or wants to see me. He has weapons
to destroy me; but I turn
the other cheek, present my other face.

Medusa Six

Self-transformation is what
makes us women:
our peculiarity, defining feature.
Watch it as girl becomes mother,
as the mother adapts to
every phase of growing in her child.

As women we discover
when to let our children go
but also when to hold and protect them.
This goes on even after we die.

The witch, the wise woman,
cannot be straitlaced.
She alone in all the world
speaks and acts without fear.
She understands the ways of maturation
and is part of the spiral of creation,
its dyings and renewals.

She can hate because she loves,
destroy because she nurtures,
performs what becomes true
avoiding all charades,
appears even ugly from wearing no mask.

She transforms herself
and cannot be confined
to one set of rules,
one pack of ideals.

Torture or condemn her,
neglect or crucify,
she will transfigure and
never leave her children comfortless.

Medusa Seven

i

Kings, presidents *naturally*
have to be in control.

A woman whose say or sway
could influence policy,
infiltrate management
of thought or emotion
is a danger *clearly*
making her man unsuitable for office.

A man whose mind is open,
whose ideas are changeable,
whose actions may not always be
predictable
is *not* someone who can stand
at the helm of the ship of state
taking orders from this side
or that: from cliques, juntas,
the party, the media, the public,
commercial magnates and
foreign investors.

ii

Look at what happened to Agamemnon.
Remember "weak" Macbeth
(as we studied his flawed character
to get through our exams).

A man like Julius Caesar
or Pontius Pilate now:
they were not sidetracked
by warning from their wives.

iii

How does a woman manage,
with her five wits and six senses,
not to be conscious of what is happening
in her husband's all-important
all-absorbing world of work?

How does she refrain from forming an opinion
or coming to a conclusion?

If she knows something significant
does she risk his anger by telling him
or risk his anger by keeping silent?

How does she abstain
from dropping the slightest hint,
commenting on events?

Is she a statue or doll?
How does a woman surrounded by fools
conceal her wisdom?

iv

Some are born great and some
have greatness thrust
(like Samson's hairy head)
into their lap.

Medusa Eight

At this late dawn
another worn tree is felled.
Hard ground of winter
receives the weight of timber
without grumbling.

The chain-saw whines.
By dark the trunk and branches
are turned into logs:
a fire to warm no-one.
Tomorrow the ashes
will be whiter than frost.

Old man, when you died
you took with you the glamour
of your righteousness and medals.

All that I was taught
in my youth to applaud
(my praises, hero-worship)
has ended with you.

We have no complaint
when a patriarch falls —
we slaves and women,
peasants and primitives.

In our poverty and bondage
we have our special orders
and grow our own gods.

Medusa Nine

We search for someone who can remember us
as baby, as little child, exuberant
ten-year-old or shy intellectual teenager
hot with hopeful ideals and cold with logic.

We know ourselves only in shadows,
pictures we've gathered and framed from
the memories of others, their stories or
shared experiences. Our reality

in the past, depends on these, as much
as on our own snatches of self-transcendance,
from letters we wrote, from people we knew
whose images are essential to our design.

We can dream of each other as young
and let ourselves play the part, even
relent and pretend we love as we did
when our ideals were free, our hopes secure.

Perhaps we can recreate for each other a memory,
relive for each other, dramatise and share,
restore the person, who otherwise slowly fades:
for lack of a past the present floating away.

Medusa Ten

It is the goddess in me when I rage,
when in lamentation
I weep, destroy, rip up, to assuage
her holy indignation
at her humiliation.
My woman's body is today her temple.
I cannot disengage
from my task as priestess and disciple.

It is she who will defend, prevent
my being put in chains,
however seriously or kindly meant;
the custom that restrains,
work that sustains
others, while her spirit slows, diminishes.
She cannot give consent
to such denial of her darling wishes.

She it is who acts when I refuse
comfort or compromise,
however justifiable the cause,
undetectable its lies.
If she is wise,
then loneliness, despair will "serve me right":
did I not have to choose
the way of darkness flowering into light?

She sings in songs of shadow and affliction,
in myths of loss and grieving
as for thousands dying of starvation,
each death bereaving
all of us, leaving
the earth, our lives, incidents again
of bombs and exploitation,
cancer in the blood, polluted rain.

The goddess in me loves, and loving knows
how hard it is to hold
the snake, the bull, the flame, and to disclose
diverse and manifold
disguises new and old
with which a man will clothe his nakedness:
dew for the rose
to keep this world in flower and fruitfulness.

Medusa Eleven

Like a volcano
savage
churned rock and foamed gases
red, compressed,
long unseen, unknown,
that surface to be stilled, cooled,
turned to stone:

Rocked by gravitational force
the magma within her would tilt and swell
as tides do,
erupt again,
cluttered, scoured,
would flow.

Some heroes farm her fertile slopes,
channel her fires and fluids.
They love and fear.
She makes, unmakes,
not once, but slowly,
over and over, the earth.

Medusa Twelve

My head or my heart is throbbing.
My head throbs and it beats in my heart.
My heart beats and throbs in my head.

I try to locate the din.
Is it the house that shakes
or the night that drums so late?

The bed rocks, the house pulses,
faster, faster.

I have to write it down, the throbbing:

the beat, the drum,
the drive, the fear,
the hate, the drill,
the keeping awake,
the listening to it,
unable to sleep,
unable to die —
or is it death that is drumming?

Life in me pounds at the dying.
I advance, like Gandhi's people,
again and again to the baton
that strikes me down.

Medusa Thirteen

Choose between me and your shadow.

Choose me and you'll know
your true, unchided child;
you'll come upon your
abounding, practical youth
who made things new as if
at his command:
you'll own your older, wisest heart
hidden in gestures you did
not learn, in acts of
unsought understanding.

Choose me as light:
your shadow will fall into place.

Exchange of Dreams

The Willows and the Vines

Alone in a garret and dying
    O the willows and the vines
a wise old woman is lying.
She frailly talks of Luxor
her station-wagon in California
listens for our footsteps
on the stairs and corridor
it must have been before the war:

    O the willows and the vines

New Year's Eve and we're dancing
    O the willows and the vines
logs in the fire enhancing
candleray and evergreen
wine, food, music, float between
our memories and losses
as we make a merry scene
each one's skull beneath the skin:

    O the willows and the vines

The *vieille dame* is ninety-one
    O the willows and the vines
in a week or two if it come,
her birthday, or will she wander
from here a little sooner?
Her mind, exact and clear,
speaks to the truth of a stranger
who calls for half an hour:

    O the willows and the vines

"You are primitive," she says
    O the willows and the vines
"How does she know?" my heart replies.
Her impending death is treasure
she offers. I stoop and gather
this diamond rough and pure
to keep in secret store
through every death that I endure:

    O the willows and the vines

Coaltits at the window
    O the willows and the vines
lambs are born in the meadow
robins flit on fences
the gray and white collie prances
at words of recognition:
life devours its pretences
as the mind undoes distances:

    O the willows and the vines

Buddha in Europe

The Buddha of Healing has come to the centre of Europe
from Japan, *le Buddha guérisseur*,
master of remedies, with his wand to dispel fear.
A thousand years ago he was carved in cypress
wood, one hand raised, palm outward
to save us all from torment of existence, fingers
tenderly curved as if to touch and gather
cries of suffering, and to transmute
them into another song, another silence of being
nothing or no-thing or no tied-up bundle
of private passion, attachment, craving, death.
On his left hand lightly rests a jar of ointment,
panacea for illusion. His eyes are closed
and yet I know they really take me in
as I stand before him in Brussels and bow to his
        reassurance.

A thousand years surviving in cypress wood
an ancient woman prays, her lips tight with grief
and Mother Theresa ailing in Calcutta
watches over the dying, a mendicant
for love, her empty bowl for ever brimming over.

The Dalai Lama is given the prize for peace
in the year the Chinese murdered their own success,
peace of great price, the kind the people pay for.
Tibetans fled their home on the heights of Earth
and brought among us their golden way of being
human, neither in haste to resist nor to forgive,
but waiting with a gesture that banishes fear
of no-good devils, however efficient.
The Dalai Lama is Buddha-Nature made manifest,
and the pearl of peace he prizes shines on his brow.

The Buddha of Healing is here in the heart of Europe.
He attracts to his palm the silent cries
of our century, offers salve of enlightenment.
It is only a tiny jar and yet if we open it
carefully, — for how can there be enought to go round? —
we find it is empty, a begging bowl, or a shining pearl.

Monks in Black and White

Monks in black and white walk through the snow:
the silence of their order broken by the creak
their bootsteps make where snow is soft and clean
and by birds who scarcely sound their notes. A robin
sings alone to mark his territory
and clustered chaffinches sit heavily upon
snow-laden boughs. Crows and gulls mark out
the black and white with equal hunger, as deep in prayer
the monks walk silently in single file.

They pray for peace while tramping through the snow.
I, too, keep silent, watch wordless weapons speak,
oil gush, bridges explode, expensive
missiles shatter hard-won lives. We quietly hood
ourselves in cowls of privacy. We wear
the whited cassock of our liberal views, and know
how hard it is to think beyond the needs
of those we love. We lie alone at night and hope
for courage in the face of every day.

To My Son Going Abroad

Abroad is the place to be in this world.
It is where we were born
and is always where we are heading.

This island is but one landing stage
on the passage-lines of the world
that voyagers know as they come to harbour.

To settle here is to nestle among the familiar
but you would explore.

You will meet subtle webs of thinking:
people who gather your thoughts
before you start to explain.

They will know your feelings too
and uncover words in their languages
for those we have hopelessly left unnamed —

and so you'll explore yourself
in that great abroad,
in heat and height and dirt and disease
and in the abundant nakedness,
revealed, of primeval earth
and its stark fragility.

If you lose your soul to explore the world,
the world will restore it again enriched
but do not lose patience:
that is the one thing necessary.

I shall practise it, too, in your absence
and expend my travelling words
plumed with it, and with love,
for your company, your comfort.

Floating People

Tides are slowly encroaching on the coast:
beaches disappear that we knew;
seaside resorts are flooded, only spires
are seen at low tide in fear.
The outline of dry land is lost and blurred.

The wise are already building boats:
new designs, experiments; they learn.
Families clear out their homes.
They teach themselves the art of navigation
and seamanship, like ancient Celtic monks.

Seasons we used to know have melted
one into another; soil is salinated;
wild flowers have no locality;
trees forfeit their rhythms and are dwindling;
only dark and light have kept their pattern.

Britons who could boast they ruled the waves
float as refugees in makeshift craft.
"Great London is no more" it is cried,
and every slight hillock is a prize
for people who would stake themselves an acre.

※ ※ ※

But who will take us in, with our bundles
of books and precious heirlooms, family albums,
pictures of where we lived: street, square,
school, shops, the park or fields?
Or with our packaged rations, ragged clothes?

The empire that we lost or gave away?
The colonies we treated as our slaves?
Tribesmen made to dance for us and starve?
Chiefs we dispossessed and thought
were not our equals, swopped their land for beads?

Our whisky rivers now are sluggish, grey;
no snow to sparkle in the summer corrie;
neglected upland terrain is thronged
with ruins of the shielings, now repaired
by those who dread the sea and foreign lands.

     ✻ ✻ ✻

Can I claim my Indian birthright and return
to that motherland of sweat and stench
whose languages speak with my tongue?
Six generations in my blood: pre-
destination, karma, chosen fate?

I'd take my children back where they were born —
but I am in their hands: I am old.
Better I should die than take up space
in this diminished world. My daughters,
my grandchild: she will work her passage.

I bequeath her my bi-national soul:
the Scottish one that seems to be familiar,
the Indian one that never lets me go.
She will sail as her ancestors did
from Clyde to Calcutta and beyond.

But she will leave without idea
of governing or earning or even
serving those she needs to live among.
"India," she will plead, "Give me refuge.
Take me as a child of your heart.

Let me work a place on your hearth,
contribute to each mouthful I consume" —
caught up in a vast exchange of peoples
to accept the wiser rulings of the east
where first shall be last, last not least.

     ✻ ✻ ✻

To you I bequeath my battered courage,
the lonely adventure of this voyage,
this subordination to the laws
of earth and sea. You shall have my talents
to scatter in the fields where you tread.

May you make abode for your children
learn the craft and lore you will need
for the next evolution of Earth.
A new human dignity arises
when all are exiles, all inhabitants.

The memories you retain of the north,
of Scotland, stones and long dark,
cold winds and clear wild skies —
these will haunt your dreams, in your blood,
as India has never ceased in mine.

*   *   *

Now we must rehearse and memorise
songs and stories of our ancestors,
for these will be our passport at the frontiers,
our pathfinders and our identity
when ports are crowded, people drowned.

Before I die I'll write down the notation
for each tune that sings in my story,
even if I know only fragments.
You will slowly learn the missing parts
from others in the fuller harmony.

Burden

Elephants of polished teak, ivory tusks,
carved by Indian *mistri* cross-legged in the dust,
wrapped in his *chadar* and carried to the station,
spread out on the platform to catch the dulled eyes
of British families travelling in May
to the hills, or returning in September
after the Monsoon . . . a few annas thrown.

The craftmanship is perfect and detailed:
one elephant pulls and the other pushes
a log of teak as big as themselves.
Mighty civil servants, the leader takes the strain
and the other puts his weight behind the task.
The white man's burden? Elephantine
to build and bridge, to heal and teach,
to manage and manufacture,
to transport and distribute.

Ships brought them to a bitter post-war Britain.
They settled as they could in villages and suburbs,
market towns and terraces, but on their mantelpieces
teak elephants were still and still at work.

Passed on to the children who had played with them
from house to house, the tusks now loose,
the burden was inherited along with carpets,
silver, jewelry.
                                       All I have is from the India
of my parents. Surrounded by it I live
far from it. Chained to the log I cannot move.

Set Loose

A company of long grey snakes
slides through child-high grassland
near Bangalore. The grasses roll
like waves but when the snakes
have passed they stand undamaged.

Children slept veiled in mosquito-nets
and on the ceiling a fan slow-whirled.
A cobra was coiled where I stood
to open the skylight, untwisting
a thin cord to let in the Indian night.
It had entered by the water-sluice
where bathtubs were emptied. Why did men
rise up from their string-beds to kill it
then and there and cover it where it lay?

They came early to bury it next morning
in case a dog should eat it and fall dead
(as if they cared about the life of dogs).
It was a ritual: snakes must be killed
even while they sleep, innocently coiled.

Now I am disentangling the ropes
that open the sky, while men
and children sleep. Now I take up
the coiled serpent with its crushed head
and set it loose to ripple through the fields.

Vineyard in Winter

In winter I find my sun
in wood my tree
in mist my horizon
    in work generative
    my swing, my liberty,
    my aimless motive.

Sleeping beneath rafters
to waken in early dark
peasants or crofters,
    it is labour of the season
    we bend but do not break
    for the body has its reason.

The *vignoble* lets me trust
the twisting intellect
cut back in frost
    resumes its long task
    through stages until perfect
    like good wine in the cask.

Heavy soil and gnarled vine
raise the tender grape
to bloom in its sheen—
    a diamond essence
    ours to drink and keep
    a deepening brilliance.

Chanticleer

Chanticleer
I hear
your notes
float
through dark
to wake
from dreams
demand
response
from sense.

You stay
never betray
your flock
or mock
at love
or leave.

I read late
in the night.
I weep
until I sleep.
Then you cry
my reveille
as if a tune
for me alone.

Laura

I did see Laura in Avignon.
It was after finding the church and cloister
where Petrarch first beheld her in 1327,
Santa Chiara, or Saint Clare in sun-drenched
yellow stone with a suggestion of garden
seen through the huge wrought-iron gate
that bars the place—for work of restoration.

The birth-point of the Renaissance
is restored to bring in money
from sentimental literary addicts,
intrigued that such a normal event
as seeing a girl in church could
trigger centuries of art.

But I saw Laura walking
up the *rue des trois faucons*.
No tourist, she walked fast and no-one
noticed her but me. Her thick hair
was swept up in a chignon.
She wore a terracotta shirt
over generous bosom,
and a swinging black skirt.

With bare legs and feet in sandals
she went briskly by and disappeared.
I do not know if my description is accurate
but the woman I saw was beautiful,
was Beauty incarnate, was Petrarch's vision.

Le *Carrousel*

Too many people who have to be fed
in Paris, say in *rue des Italiens*
or *quatre Septembre*. Too many brasseries
and cafes and restaurants and hotels
and pizza houses and steak houses and
too many faces from all the nations
eating as much as they can afford
which is more than is good for them.

Duck and goose and lamb and beef and chicken and veal—
did you see the day-old calf on the mountain terrace,
already able to dance away from the tongue
of its mother and flick its ears?
Young heifers are made to fight at Arles
in the Bull-Ring: they are fiercer.
Vachettes they are called,
a delicacy for enjoyment, like *escalopes de veau*.

* * *

Tall avenues of trees line the tomb-way
at Alicamps, where we pay to promenade.
A young woman sits on a grave
to feed her week-old baby,
a white parasol for shade.
The stained-glass chapel window is covered
in cobwebs and dust is thick on the friezes
in the well-preserved Augustinian cloister.

Look at the food: huge grapes and melons,
enormous marrows and pumpkins,
fish and meat and mussels and oysters
and massive cheeses, barrels of butter.

Look at the clothes: slinky and sparse,
a month's wages for a jacket,
a week's for a leather belt—
and most of the garments worthless,
not comfortable or lasting or
protective or fitting.
A name tag is their fortune.

Who are the people who buy these clothes,
eat this food? In cars they rape
the narrow lanes of ancient cities.
On motorbikes they ejaculate noise.
In the *Promenade des Papes*
we are flattened against the walls.

*   *   *

Up in the mountains we beg a few eggs
from the neighbours. We pick brambles
and apples and tomatoes, the fruit
of back-breaking labour making
terraces in the rock, tending,
watering from underground,
climbing, digging, weeding, learning
the needs and loves of the plants.

There are crowds at *Barbes Rochechouart*
so thick on the pavement at *Tatis*
they hardly move. They chat and
jumble through baskets of sellable stuff:
clothes of all colours, toys, household goods
they are called. We have given up
household *gods*. Those we must make
ourselves, with our own hands
in silence and night vigils.

*   *   *

The food is all piled up in Paris
and Brussels and Amsterdam and London
and Frankfurt – places with names we see
on boards lit-up at airports,
where busloads of tourists descend
to be entertained and guided
through visions of the past.

The woman and child still stand for life
carved vulnerably on corners of buildings
and gargoyles wait, opposing,
as if about to spring.
But the popes have familiar faces,
betraying obvious human foibles,
and poor Van Gogh lived in misfortune
in Arles for only a year.
One lark above the vineyard!

We cannot lift the tools and implements
of our fathers, the fishhooks or ploughs
or axes. We cannot reach the distant mountains
where they built their homes, where no road leads.

*   *   *

The carrousel rotates in the square with music and lights.
It is strongly-built of fine wood,
carved and painted, with stairs to an upper level.
Horses and coaches and elephants
undulate, circulate.
It slows; it stops; we have to come down.
How much did we pay for three minutes?
How shall we spend our life-span?

Thunder in Vaucluse

(September 1992)

Thunder on the ramparts and
lightning across the slate-dark sky
in ziggurats.

Old cedars lean on their supports
and peacocks peck about in flooded grass
around the sundial calendar.

We cannot tell the time today
adding two hours for man-made
adjustments. It is the equinox.

Yesterday the people decided *oui ou non*
to bring the world more naturally together
or to remain in age-old artificial blocks.

By three per cent they voted *yes*
but this thunder is their own,
particularly, passionately French.

The crack of thunder follows us
into a cafe and looks into mirrors.
We have nowhere to hide.

Up in the mountains a car is swept away
and a farmer has been killed when
he went to save his horses.

Rivers have flooded and havocked
the systems of precarious city life.
Renaults and Citroëns are tossed and driven.

The bent Augustinian clock tower
in Avignon, the medieval walls
and the massive Papal Palace

are not crushed by thunder-storm
or lightning or time or disbelief or traffic
or tourists or the sorrow of erosion.

The great Roman aqueduct does not fall
while the undergound fountain at Vaucluse
slowly fills to torrent down its boulders.

Another thunder crash and huge drops
of rain attack the ornamental pool
where goldfish skiddle skaddle.

It is the vote, the equinox, the storm.
We must decide. We are not fish or trees.
We make our principles, our monuments.

We voice, we decide, we know
we have no choice. The earth
has sworn by water, air and fire.

Rose Window, Vincennes

The form of the rose is fire
wreaths of flame like tendrils
grow from the coiled heart

flame forms the heart
fiery tendrils coil
to wreath the growing rose

tendrils grow in wreaths
the heart a coil of fire
the rose a form of flame

wreath formed of fire
tendrils grown from flame
the heart of the coiled rose

the rose grows a wreath
the heart forms tendrils
that coil and flame and fire

grow flaming rose
tendrils wreath and coil
form the fiery heart.

Exchange of Dreams

On the visa card a mini-scene
of mountains and "Is ziss Loch Ness?"
asked the waitress in Paris.
"I ev a dream to go zhere."

"Perhaps it is Loch Ness,"
we peer at the piece of plastic
to find her depth of vision
that money cannot buy.

Suddenly we wonder why
we dreamt of coming to Paris.
Did we glimpse a picture
of the Elysian Fields?

Golden Images

Please leave this mask of gold upon the skull
the buried gold, fast-plated to the corpse.

In the name of science don't strip it off
or tear apart the body and its sheath

of treasures, ornaments and familiar
daily objects, belongings that were used
for ritual, sacred totems we worshipped.

While ancient peoples buried works of art,
statuary, jewelry, airless and untouched,
alone, unseen around a royal corpse

we shoot our wealth to space, to the illustrious
moon, or blow it up in bombs made of the sun.

What is the empty mask, the golden mould
detached from the corpse it was designed for?

It is a shell to be wondered at, admired
for craftsmanship, commercial tradery.

We try to live by images alone and cast
aside the mortal person, the decay.

A photograph is all we cling to now
for we have buried what was real in the heart.

No one can excavate the treasure there,
steal through the wings of goddesses or across
the silent forepaws of the guardian hound,

who sepulchre my memories and keep
them safe-preserved and gleamingly attached
to the actual person, to the ones I love,
whether they are living yet or dead.

Rough Bounds

Rough Bounds

Leaps and bounds as the river
as sure-footed mountain deer
as rock forms barrier

Rough and ready as hill track
as long standing drystane dyke
as stepping stones surely mark

The shallow place we cross over
the pass worn by wayfarers
marking the natural order

Bounds and bonds we shake loose
forsake or have to sacrifice
on the destiny we choose

Universals of our planet
circumference to starry orbit
perfect each within its limit

Out of bounds we take the risk
questions each one has to ask
to go beyond may be our task

Boundless as in exaltation
the lark sings, or lamentation
that brooks no consolation

Silence then, free of words
forward then where is no guide
rough bounds within my head.

Viewpoint

*Why can't they give these damn mountains
proper names?* Their names are
in our language. The mountains
understand it and know each other
by these proper Gaelic names.

*Why can't they be spelt so we can
pronounce them? – like Ben Nevis
or Ring of Bright Water?*
The spelling is the way it works
and makes everything real.

*I can't remember these names.
What does "Sgurr" mean?*
Steep, high, impenetrable peak
that divides our minds, our speech
and our understanding.

Here's one I can say: Ben Tee.
And here is Gleouraich, Gairich,
Spidean Mialach, Sgurr na Ciche.

(Mist and clouds are swirling
as an eagle soars and falls).

*What is that range called, that
you see and then it fades?*
Knoydart. It means Rough Bounds!
Dear, far, near, fearsome
rough bounds of our being.

The Shetland Fiddler

The Shetland fiddler moves neither
head, shoulders, hair, eyes, mouth;
expressionless and rigid as
rocks that do not jump about
contain the dark dancing
of the waters of the voe.

The fiddle does not move, only
bow and bowing arm, and fingers
urgent on the strings. The music
moves, the player but an instrument.

So keeps the Buddha still and Francis
who prayed "Make me an instrument."

The Clarsach

In a clarsach there are no verticals
or horizontals
only diagonals and curves.
The straights are on the slant
and the curves on the level.
That is the thing about it—
this intersection of movement.
But the clarsach is no thing,
it is an instrument,
perfect as such before
the player touches it
with our human music.

Carried Away

In January 1886 Betty Mouat, an elderly spinster from Shetland, was the only passenger on The Columbine, *a clipper taking shawls to be dressed in Lerwick, when the captain was knocked overboard in a gale. The two-man crew tried unsuccessfully to rescue him in the dinghy and could not get back to the ship. Betty Mouat drifted alone for eight days and nights until the boat was washed ashore on a rocky island beach off Norway.*

Like Jonah in the whale   I found myself swallowed alive
Alone in the ship's bowels   the crew gone overboard
Caught in a northern gale   sailsheets ripped through their hands.

I heard them thump and shout.   I heard them lower the dinghy.
I heard the wild sea attack   lurch and rap the vessel.
The ladder fell from the hatch   sealed me into the tomb

Of the cabin, darkness, damp,   everything flung around
That wasn't made fast or fixed –   my head, my body, free
To be thrown and battered   until I roped and tethered myself.

That was the first darkness   after I'd howled and moaned
To recognise I was doomed   no one could rescue me
My horse without rider, my ship,   unlikely to finish the course.

When winter light returned   most precious drops of day
I stood on a chest to look out   at the desolate wilderness
My loose-reined vessel astray   in black and swirling seas.

I found the skipper's watch   hung on a nail in the cabin
Wound it and set it to tell the time   as I judged by light.
Time was my company,   my piece of the human world.

Snow and hail and rain   and spray coming down the hatch
Cold and wet and my feet numb   no longer my own
I came on the skipper's jacket   to comfort my bruised bones.

For lack of food and sleep   my thinking was erratic
I did what meant survival   action directed thought
Hour after hour of dark   I gazed at familiar stars.

The Columbine herself was alone   and about to die
Was thrown and tossed and battered
                              and blown and shattered by breakers
Unaware of her destination   helpless to make direction.

I was her living heart   her questioning, conscious mind
I was the tiny, frail,   accidental fragment
That made her more than flotsam   and jetsam upon the ocean.

She and I were bonded   into a new-formed creature
No fish or sea-born mammal,   no weapon or man-made object
Together we made a new whole,   woman and boat as one
Lending each other a curious   immortal identity.

*   *   *

Compass reading uncertain   I try to focus my thoughts
Gather the yarn and firmly   spin the thread of my days
On the wheel the wheel the wheel   how do I keep it turning –

Moisten my lips with spray   succumb to dull starvation
Draw from my stored resources   body tissue and memory
Daze and dream and weep   and keep myself awake –

For asleep I will be crushed   in the sea's rough cradling
And the finest shawls ever made   bundles of them beside me
Could not wrap   or protect me from that racking.

The Columbine   she must practise her acrobatics now
With no applause or spectators   ride the sea bareback
Let her prance dance   cavort somersault

Pretend to fall to falter   to faint keep still and die
But rise again with a laugh   to perform another trick
And see it all as harmless   a jape a harlequinade.

What other way to live?   What other explanation
For counterpoint of loss?   With hope and happiness
The skipper drowns   and he a seaman who could swim

A strong man   schooled by hardship and the sea
A man who seemed   as if death could have no dominion
Over him, his powers –   a man to be trusted

With ships for sailing   cargoes, shawls and precious knitting
A husband and father   a son and brother –
The two young men, his crew,   did they make it home?

Young men grow faint   and their knees very feeble
The infirm survive   who no longer seek to
My lameness my greyness   my sadness my loneliness...

                      *   *   *

And the shawls we knitted   taken to be treated
In Lerwick for the market   intricated pattern
Like lace but wool   fine spun a refinement.

Our fingers and our tongues   talking and knitting
But no mistake made   that was not at once corrected
No idle gossip   but eager accurate –

The stories we believe   the lives we spin
the relationships we weave   the loves we knit
But I somehow alone   my mother's only child

My father's only daughter   before he was drowned
This is a sure way   to find again my father
The everlasting arms   the eternal waves.

It is strange to be apart   but part of a community
As close as ours   each one related
But I am separate   and alone I sail

Towards my death any moment   my death   how many days?
The waters invade the ship   will sink   how many nights?
Dark   it is loud   seascape shouts with dark.

No stars again tonight   shall I see the sun
Once more before the end?   Shall I be forgiven
For hardness of heart   for pride in my talents

For keeping love ashore   not letting it drift
On the waves and be drowned   be surfaced and stranded
For holding love dry   for the deprivation?

Shall I be forgiven   for lack of indulgence
For prudence and thrift   for supporting myself
And teaching the young   and helping my neighbour?

This is my punishment   driven out to sea
Sent into exile   banished by the wind
Lost in the distance   floating the fathoms

Taken to sea in a storm   of love in brain in hands
The sails of it torn from my holding   my body thrown
To the waves   but chained   confined   solitary
As I travel I know not where   and against my will.

*   *   *

Mother I love you   Mother where are you
Mother and Father I'm calling you   calling –
My voice can't be heard   I am in the womb.

Let me be born   as daylight returns
I am born each time   I emerge through the hatch
the companionway   and I see rocks   a red light.

Today I see land   land means hope   eight days old
But also danger   rocks will strike and gouge
Timbers will scrape and crack   I cannot guide her.

Someone may see me   before I lose consciousness
I must be visible   climb on deck
lie like a seal awaiting the guns   be seen

Must prove I am who I am   unwise old woman
determined child   competent clever in control
quietly me   reliable brave.

No one complains of me   nor I of them
I don't want to make a fuss   Why should I hope to be saved?
Why should I exist and why   why should I die?

People lift me   strong men take me
Now I can faint now I can sleep   now I can drift
Now I can sail away   *The Columbine* crashes and breaks

On the rocks on the island shore   the land
Destroys what the sea could not   now I must
Leave her   my womb   tomb   my floating chrysalis
I am her soul departing   for I have arrived.

Travelling on Music

The car runs on music
and needs to be conducted
rather than driven.
It varies tempo and theme
to the kind of country it crosses.

Hear it surge along the motorway
to Beethoven's ninth,
wind along riversides
to the floating continuous
glide of his violin concerto,
or dance between hedgerows
to Mozart's clarinet,
soar up over hills and topple into a panorama
with full orchestration.

We stop for a coffee between movements,
but music drives us on
until the *adagio* brings us homeward
on strings, not wheels,
and we silently come to rest.

To The Swift

They used to bind his knees, he was so swift—
and some have held themselves in check afraid
their strength would take them out of reach
of friends or family—and some
have concealed in pots and pans,
stifled in laundry, squandered in shopping,
scaled down to child-size their energy and talent.

With knees bound, did he lose his prowess,
or forget it was his? If suddenly
someone released him, would he run,
run and leap along the strand, over the hills
for the joy of it,
unafraid of envy, prepared to confess:
I have this power,
I am this speed, this creature
that runs so fast is me.

Or would he go on hobbling at the pace
his peers ordained, the average speed,
safe and comfortable, companionable,
no longer able to believe himself
a runner, "the swift one"?

But see, he has a child.
She cannot eat for the need to run
and run. The child grows thin
with distance and the loneliness.
Should he bind the knees of his child
for her own good, as his had been?

He tells his daughter of Achilles
and the choice he had of brief life
with glory or a long life with none.
"If you run ahead," he warned her,
"You will wait for others to catch up

which they will never do. They will try
to trip you up and hold you back.
They will despise your tales
of what you see on untried ways.
You will take the risk alone
and take the blame and take,
perpetually, the disappointment
and apparent failure. Glory
will not reward you either.
That is reserved for the satisfactory."

"I will run," the child replied,
and paused and added,
"but I will run back again
and then ahead. To and fro
I'll keep in touch. And I'll keep quiet
about what I discover, except
to those who ask the right questions."

Her father watched her go
faster and faster into the distance,
where a light shone and enveloped her.
He stretched his knees, then fell on them
to pray. His daughter did return,
but she kept the secret of her speed
and never let it lapse. She knew
she must surpass herself to live
and that she must return—
that *returning* is the bondage
of the swift.

The Wall and the Tree

*In India, when a tree is growing through a wall,
it is the wall that must come down.*
         —Kathleen Raine, *India Seen Afar.*

Said the Wall to the Tree: "You may grow close to me.
I'll give you shelter from spiteful weather.
Nothing can budge me, bend me or break me.
I stand my ground. Firmly founded
from time immemorial, I'm territorial.
I know what belongs. I keep right from wrong
and divide up the country, protecting property –
an effective sign of the Mine and Thine.
Beside me," said the Wall, "you never will fall."

The seedling Tree accepted gratefully
the Wall's kind offer of effective cover
from heat or cold, wind and wild
animals. Young leaves and petals
shone in the Spring. The trunk was stretching
taller, roots down, branches wider.
Stone by stone it was seen to have grown
each year until it emerged, joyful,
in its own strength, settled in earth.

The Tree leaned over the Wall, looking beautiful,
its flowers cascading, leaves fluttering,
its roots creeping downward, deep.
At last it was clear the Wall was in peril:
"Hurry up and remove it. Do I have to prove it?
My stones are looser, my pointing and mortar
are crumbling. The Tree is pushing
me from below. It will have to go."

The Tree bent to console the threatening Wall,
touched the stones with leaves, in winter thrown
by winds at its feet. Birds would flit
from branch to Wall and back. People
rested and talked. But then they hacked
the Tree to pieces. They knew their business.

Parable

The tree longed for the day
when she could cease bearing fruit.

year after year all her energies
went into fruit production.

It was as if root and branch,
stem, bud, leaf and flower

had no other talent or potential
than toiling to make fruit, –

the burden of it, the weight,
and the never-ending labour.

"If only," thought the tree,
"I could use my roots to study something in depth,

My leaves to be creative
in other ways: dance, music, poetry.

I wish I could exist for my own sake
and play my full part in global ecology."

At last the time came
when the tree was no longer fruitful.

She shuddered with terrible ecstasy,
knew herself essential and beautiful.

Autumn came. The tree was lightsome,
shed a profusion of brilliant ideas.

But the farmer was no fool:
"useless," he decided, and felled her.

An Easter

Easter in Scotland means East wind
hurtling over the hills and along
stony High Streets of county towns.

Lambs shudder, huddle for shelter
in hollows or under rocks. Daffodils
brave it out in park and churchyard.

Nature does her best to keep faith
with Life, provides her buds and blossoms,
her birds nesting beside the river.

The swan is shining among the reeds,
coiled in her nest, and curlews cry
in circles above their grassy nurseries.

The river is black and flows with winter's
ferocity, despite primroses
and grey wagtails in matching yellow.

We climb to the Holy Cairn up a muddy
track and stand in the bitter wind
at an altar face of broken boulders.

They guard the womb where the dead
were placed in foetal position
to be reborn. It makes an Easter.

Evensong (May)

Outline of the hill clear against a pale silver sky.
Dusk hovers, birds sing acutely and, far below, the river
winds from one cluster of village lights to the next.

Cherry blossom in the churchyard. Willows and alders
boughed with pale green leaves. Black and white cows
moan and sway on their way to the drinking place.

One squared green field is dotted white with lambs
and next to it the graveyard rectangles. This old
hill fort invisibly commands the merging valleys.

I clamber on its rocks and sense the landscape
as if it rolled up its present habitations and
returned to the contours it has held over aeons.

When I descend and reach our gate I see you
in the lighted window-frame asleep. I come in
and close the curtains before the stars appear.

I know that they are there above the tallest trees
and that grey wagtails, like moonbeams,
are nesting by the river.

Winter Day in the Borders

Leaves are falling singly in the mist.
Grasses, still unwithered, on the old hill-fort
are decorated separately in frost.

A dog treads water in a pool of leaves.
A motor-cycle growls in the forest,
its rider clad for jousting against the gradient.

Above the bristly hill a cool moon.
The river fiercely tosses white water backwards
over rocks and seething stoic depths.

The dipper dances on a fallen log
in syncopation, chirping to its mate, loud
above the skimming surface of the flow.

The wide moorland circles round the village
protected by its cold, covering wind.
An owl flies, crying in the dusk.

Pines lean against the snow-dark sky.
Stiff with silent fishing, a heron flaps
into their high branches. We turn home.

First Thaw

Hills lie quilted in snow;
the river runs black and harsh;
sheep are fed by hand.

Next day a flicker of doves
streams over the rooftops, the church
and circles down to the river.

A sprinkle of snowdrops beside the flood
and a pair of dippers play dive and seek.
The heron flies low upstream.

A cat crouches on the wall
which sparkles with favoured moss.
A girl leads her pony along the street.

We walk slowly arm in arm
over the bridge, along the river
and imagine ourselves in the picture.

Gorse Girl

My gorse girl
dazzling pale
quine o' the whin
scorns to smile

Gold effulgence
brutal thorns
the suffering
that builds a crown

From your nature –
delicate, sharp,
sheer, enduring –
no escape

It will keep you
growing wild
in wind and sun
in rain and cold

You will make
your scented flowers
appear again
they will resurge

in bold abundance
to brand the hill
with spreading brilliance
fiery girl

A *Scented Garden*

Peebles has a scented garden
"for the blind," planted beside the river
opposite the modern swimming pool.

Unblind, I close my eyes to breath
and listen: a linnet is singing
in lemon-scented leaves.

I imagine orange blossom with roses,
frangipani and hyacinth.
East and west are met in the scented garden.

Blindly I aquiesce. My east and west,
synthetic, abolish the dualities
that sight imposes on our world.

The river chants its plainsong.
I open my eyes. You are watching me, smiling.
I take your hand and lead you down the street.

Working Mind

The Tweed flows, fierce and quiet
(like an engine in top gear).
It sweeps up reeds, trees
and devours its own banks.
A half moon is outlined
high in the south-east, clear,
although it is midday
and February's sun is low.

I work on the magazine,
read poems of modern China
accompanied by radio jazz
"the dark town-strutters' ball."
My mind flows like the river –
fast: it quietly races
under a midday moon
devouring its own banks.

Slow Emotion

Poetry Goes Through Walls

Poetry goes through walls of brick
or stone or mud or any
solid, visible substance.
What's hard in that?
A slender plant can do it.

Walls of silence – they are the test –
or walls we face on parting,
the seven-walled city of loneliness,
which even Joshua and all those ram's horns sounding
could not have broken down.

Poetry goes through walls:
the insubstantial ones that cannot
have anything pinned or painted on them,
graffiti written in air.

Antigone!
No one shall ever again
be walled up alive. You made
poetry and it goes through walls.

Carmina Gadelica in Australia

Shipped out a hundred years ago
with Scottish island exiles
like them to seek its fortune,
the book was shelved in the university
of Sydney, while they farmed the Outback.

There it was deserted, dusty, unseen,
unrecognised, while they cut down trees,
raised cattle, sheep and children,
endured two world wars.

Les Murray came upon it and
slit the pages with his penknife
to read himself into a world
where poetry was the language of people,
their way with nature in its wildness
within them and without,
the tides of light and darkness
surging over grains of sand,
each fragile human being.

He cut the pages of his own locked life:
a hundred years of hardship and hardihood
far from the sea, and now a tide of words
in and out of old country and new,
a sea he could bathe in and come ashore
in himself, wild with words.

Force Fields

In Rockall I am cradled
caressed in Finisterre

From Faroes distantly
a hundred songs are rising

Martin and Forth
I gather myself
Viking and Cromarty
dance and dare me
Fisher and Dogger
fathom and ground me

Ancestral voices from Hebrides
and Shannon – falling

Within Fair Isle I am dreamed
within Fastnet I'm decided

Finally take Sole:
the breezes are moderate—
I am the gale.

Navigare necesse est, Vivere non est

To Navigate is essential, to Live is not

The seagull hunger invaded my heart
a hunger for nothing known or lost
but for the stars and a sure
means of navigation.

To navigate is all the skill
a life can need: when to keep on course
is to hold the tiller of daily decisions
referring to the constant constellations
deep within skies of memory and longing,
immovable in the sway of emotion's compass.

To live is mere survival –
slight chance in a wreckage.
To navigate is essential:
to face in the right direction.

Transverberation

Sequence of seven sonnets

I

I know you do not speak of what you fear
for fear I would protect you from doing
what you want: to go on enjoying
our curiously happy adventure.
We work and we know we must not tire,
ceaselessly making what is beautiful
without reward, unhurriedly, until
the poetry itself is our desire.

I know your sadness is well-disciplined,
but would not have you put it from your mind:
you are completed by its presence –
nor do you turn aside when I am weeping.
Let's walk on through the woods. Your hand is keeping
mine warm in your pocket, talking nonsense.

II

My hand in your pocket talking nonsense
or perhaps in touch with all that's wisest
in the world of energies, and closest
to reality: without pretence.
Nerves and skin, distributors of essence,
inform and form us. My hands take their shape
from ancestors, their life-work, like landscape
in fields that yield their ploughed-in resonance:

The captain who sailed to Australia
with wife and children in a paddle steamer,
surgeon, teacher or administrator.
Artist and engineer combine in me:
I know the strains of each one's destiny
and your voice acts now as their arbiter.

III

Your voice acts now as my arbiter,
not by words you utter but the generous
tone and grain, precise yet sensuous,
that designs the rashness of your nature.
What conducts our voices? The heart or
the tremors of the earth? Before we speak
we hear. In some language our minds awake:
Gaelic, Hindi, English, father, mother.

Our voice forms through language, lends it colour,
the most personal and peculiar
of our attributes, need never grow old.
Unique, and yet in voices we relate,
share ourselves, sympathise, intimate.
Love through our voices will not be concealed.

IV

Love through our voices cannot be concealed
nor is it absent in our silences.
I understand your subtle defences
and what you did not mean when you smiled.
Scenes from the past may suddenly unfold
in the midst of some normal daily task.
We do not have to mention them, or ask
what is too complicated to be told.

I hear you on the telephone and wonder
how our voices fly to one another
O for the wings, for the wings of a dove:
our disembodied words will columbine,
reach home where the codings intertwine—
Then we say "I love you" and have to laugh.

V

We say "I love you" and have to laugh:
It is absurd, we know, and equally
we know it is essential. Tenderly
to live for one another is enough.
I watch you as a birch tree, silvery,
straight, elegant, reliable and tough
in all weathers, yet you are desirous of
my ministration, almost gallantly.

Love is a protection that exposes
us to greater loneliness. In a world
too small and yet too large for the human
we crave the landscape of beloved faces.
Familiar paths and features guide and lead
us bravely onward with our eyes open.

VI

We are led onward with our eyes open—
and yet we notice what we imagine
only, or learn to see. We determine
our world as we would have it happen.
We choose, it seems, perhaps we intervene,
in search of law and beauty, a garden
of our making, a down-to-earth Eden
to grow, evolve, as it has always done.

We have come together now and have changed
our key to harmonise with one another
bringing into play a latent person
who had no voice or who was a stranger
to us: as if an angel visitor
unrecognised until we pay attention.

VII

Unrecognised until we pay attention
to the unutterable voice we hear
all our lives: the music of our mother
from the womb, when we were in gestation.
In our every word we try to answer
with counterpoint, a conversation
of sound and meaning, a tradition,
which holds, breaks and redefines the measure.

Love through our voices will not be concealed,
although you do not speak of what you fear—
to live for one another is enough.
We listen and the pattern is revealed
of poetry itself, our one desire,
the task and the adventure of our love.

Slow Emotion

In Japan it is important
not to cut across the pebbles
that represent a river,
not to walk on the grass
because it is moss,
not to forget for a moment
that life is a game
with elaborated rules,
which, however, should be played
as if to win, as if it were no game,
best taken in photographs
to be experienced again
in slow emotion
albumised and still,
yet still with us
like the ancestors, gods,
dragons, the seasons.

Shiatsu

Pressure to release pressure:
stroke, stroke, press
over again harder,
tread the same ground
with thumbs and fingers
heel of hand and elbows
feet probe deeper.

As *Shado* artist
awakens the brush,
sends it on the journey
and brings it to conclusion—
so through *Shiatsu*
each rapid stroke
designs the body's signature.

B*lack* H*ara*

Black Hara absorbs light
is silence
behind any ripple of words.

The monk who sells trinkets and smiles
with a cigarette at the temple gate
has Black Hara.

The black carp swims close to the surface
in the temple lake and nudges
blood-red maple leaves
stripped from me and strewn
on the chequered water.

Kamakura

The bronze Daibutsu was sheltered
by a giant temple, but the wind took it.
They built another. A century later
it fell in a storm and a third time.
On the fourth attempt the sea itself arose
in grey pearly windswept silk
and swirled away the temple in its bosom.

They had covered the huge figure in plated gold
but sun and wind and rain and snow
of a thousand and one years
has polished it away.

Nothing can be attached to the Buddha
for he wants nothing.
Earthquakes cannot touch him but a flower can
or a bowl of oranges.
He is massive, exposed, silent, unmoving.
He is now. He is present. He is a house,
a mountain, an emptiness, a completion.

Sanjusangendo

This temple in Kyoto houses one thousand and one statues of the goddess, Kannon. It was founded in 1164. There are thirty-three bays in which the life-size statues are displayed. The central statue has eleven faces and a thousand arms.

        Thousands file past
        past the statues
        statues gilded
        gilded with multiple
        multiple arms
        arms and heads
        heads for each person
        person within us
        us and each one

        each one searches
        searches her self
        herself the goddess
        goddess of mercy
        mercy a thousand
        a thousand and one
        one is all
        all is her own
        her own beauty
        beauty that's equal
        equal to thousands

Brave

Make me brave.
Make me a brave.
Put feathers in my headdress,
beadwork at my belt.
Clothe me in a thick skin.
Arm me with a spear,
supple bow and arrows.

Enemies may come by night
and prowl into my dreams.
I'll be on my guard.
My cries will deter them.

They may come on horseback,
gallop into my mind.
I'll take steady aim
and swiftly bring them down.

Should they come offering gifts
as they used to do
when they won me over,
I'll summon my tribe of energies
to tie them to trees.

That will be the time
for poisoned arrows,
and I myself
shall wield the machete.

Caprice

Let all the prancing men be sent away:
their curved encased legs and
lithe arms, their necks that spin
and lips that sneer to make them
smile while they twist and leap.

Let the wrestlers and beef-eaters be
dismissed: their bulk deposited
elsewhere beyond my sight. Let
the rugged fighters, stalwart
battlers, compact athletes be gone.

Let the runners, hunters and hurlers
be released and take with them the
dilettantes and flabby bureaucrats.
As goddess I have chosen whom I need:
three dancing goats with horns entwined

from the age of Capricorn, Mesopotamia,
in silver, gold and bronze. Statuette.
Such is the wise man, certain of his
practices, sure in word and deed, serious,
appraising, advising and amusing.

Not *in a* Garden

(the poem refers to the Jesuit poet-priest
Gerard Manley Hopkins)

For some the agony is not in a garden:
the voice of the priest reading aloud
could be heard above the clatter of silent eating
and commotion of private misery, as novices,
spiritually battered, won through to almost the end
of another day. It was an account by Sister Emmerich,
who fled massacre in France a century before,
telling of "The Agony in the Garden."
He began to shake with sobs and left the table,
his crust uneaten. In this human crush isolated,
unable to talk, write, think, dovetail poetry.

Today he'd received a letter, opened by the Jesuit Fathers,
from Robert Bridges concerning poetry:
Your theory of *inscape* eludes me.
Pull the petals off a flower, fell an elm
and show me where "that being indoors each one dwells."
Gerard could not reply. He had written the one letter
permitted in a month, to reassure his mother
his health did not suffer from fasting or flagellation.
It did suffer, he did not tell her, from
"discipline of the eyes" keeping them downcast
so as not to see the colours of the kestrel
or clouds in whorls of crimson.

He had burnt his poems: "The Slaughter of the Innocents,"
his children, his yield like the trees'.
Not remorselessly, but relentlessly, he had killed them.
Cut open a brain and where is memory?
Where is the sense of beauty and the faculty
that responds to inscape, – those "dearest
freshness, deep down things" – call it by codename
grace or christ or soul or sakti or morphic
field, implicate order, individuation?

We glide in and out of our inscape
like a camera focusing and, sharp, we become
ourselves and poems sheer off our wings
like light on water, heedless, effortless,
bird in the dawn beyond the mist.

But among the olives his sweat like blood,
his friends unconscious and it went on,
hour after hour, with the cup forced to his lips
until he gave in, took in, let in, the violation
of death invading life.

What else shall be sacrificed?
Nine altars, passive, tall in solid stone,
now a ruin in stately gardens
at Fountains Abbey built right over the river.
Nine altars for the Virgin, or the
three-times triple goddess, whose
name is unmentionable, it is too holy.
Deleted from history and untied from religion,
she pours her tincture, a cruse of
all that adheres yet changes and has its inscape
without paring – excess is not enough.

For some the agony is not in a garden:
for the Kurdish woman who flees to the mountains,
her children barefoot in sleet, her husband killed,
her baby pushing for birth and she stumbles
in terror. Gunmen at her back, no help,
no food or shelter. Innocents slaughtered
and woman's crucifixion to be with child,
with her children and unable to save them,
yet knowing herself appointed a Guardian of Life.

Nine altars   cut open a brain   he shook with sobs
and left the table   it went on hour after hour
in this human crush isolated   unable to save them
what else shall be sacrificed?

What More

The woman stood, her hand upon her mouth
and then she broke, stumbled, ran, ran
with her tears, arms stretched out.
He saw her dwindle, tiny, no more than
a speck, until she disappeared. The train
carried him off. At first the sudden slam
of pain was all he knew. But then—
to deal with it—he hated her. Obscene
to let her heart be torn from her like that: the shame.

To let her heart be torn from her like that?
What could she do? She bore within her body
those she loved; that is the way she's made
for nurturing, so that they unfold slowly.
No need to rip, to break her suddenly
in order to escape; rather to have
become entire themselves gradually—
now she also dwells in them. To leave
by force violates, undoes the fragile weave.

They bear each other, embody one another.
It is the human way. It is mature:
the child is also father and the mother
lies like a child asleep upon the floor
of every psyche. Woman is a door –
way open, no need to break it down.
What image is impressed for ever more?
He hated her. How could he have known?
He saw the heart torn from her. What could she have done?

Regeneration

Regeneration is what counts.
Like a flower newly crushed
I'll lay aside superfluous wants
and turn the way of all plants
that look for light, however pushed
away, thrown out, displaced, torn,
I shall be centred on the sun.

Perfume is not diminished when
petals are crushed or desiccated.
Colours are as clear and clean
although leaf and stem are broken
and the plant is mutilated.
Earth accepts such limitations,
protects, restores her creations.

Vermin creep from captivity
to use the plant for their needs.
It is broken, lacks beauty,
why weep with slow pity
over withered, tangled weeds?
The huge scuttling cockroach
squats with his entourage.

The butterfly is absent now
and bees have accomplished
their work before dark. Below
ground begins renewal
of the livelihood that perished.
It is not visible. I die.
Another life begins, not I.

Shrine

Love is not a landscape we can change.
It abides within the implicate order
folded out of our sight and range
to manifest in part, in places,
to the unwithheld observer.

As continents move from the turbulent
energies we weld into firmament
of time and space, we want to arrange
the boundless, trap it and gather
up its fragments; the white tiger
is tamed, the serpent speared; danger
given a shrine, a landscape, beloved faces.

Driving Through Tweeddale

To drive through country is not to belong
and yet a sense of belonging grows
season by season, year by year. Some
horses will graze in the same meadows.
Coated in winter they droop and hang
their heads through rain and snows
but in April they put their heads together
then startle, shy, suddenly canter.

A foal spreads out asleep in the sun.
Nearby a cutter scoops up grass
and it falls like rain, green,
sweet. The foal will wake and prance.
Cattle are resting deliberately in
the mud they've made near the watering place.
Lamblife outplays a cruel April,
a hard rain, to bask in May and revel.

Two oyster-catchers nest beside the burn.
Uncamouflaged they catch my eye quickly,
and a kestrel carelessly performs, turns
in his balance, keeps it, keeps it perfectly,
but I've passed before he drops. Hawthorn
is agleam in the green with lilac
and yellow broom and bluebell-patches
beside the water's silver, and silver birches.

Plovers rise and settle their crested
heads among humps and tufts,
and wagtails flicker bright-breasted
across the road. But where are the swifts
and sand martins? Sky is dull, quiesced,
solid without them, the river bereft,
for they arrived in demolishing rain and cold:
sandbanks flooded. Nearly all died.

To drive through country is a kind
of treachery. My mother had a pony
at most, but ambled downhill to find
cowslips by the weir, or cycled stony
footpaths. Protected, I'm trapped inside
the car. I cannot touch. Only
I am touched. These presences flow,
groove into me deeply, even as I go